FRESH AIR IN THE ATTIC

FRESH AIR IN THE ATTIC

Welcome Makeovers for 7 Classic Quilts

EDITED BY *Tricia Brown*

PHOTOGRAPHY BY *Trish Reynolds*

QUILTS BY THE COLUMBIA RIVER PIECEMAKERS QUILT GUILD
FEATURING THE FABRICS OF CLASSIC COTTONS

WESTWINDS PRESS®

ACKNOWLEDGMENTS

WestWinds Press® gratefully acknowledges its appreciation to these talented quilters for their participation: Donna Adams, Pam & Ray Adams, Joyce Beckman, Roxanne Besmehn, Evaline Bixby, Tricia Brown, B. J. Clevenger, Nikki Davis, Mary Ann Emerson, Katie Garman, Linda Gilchrist, Lily Goodwin, Kathie Harris, Lorrie Hulsopple, Kay Lockwood, Cathy Lundberg, Cindy Matzen, Amanda McFeron, Edna Morse, Jean Musick, Lorrie Obermeier, Nellie Harmon Oliver, Eula Oyala, Heather Schlag, Susan Spain, Chris Stansbury, Ruthanne Tarter, Judy Teal, Marlene Van Tassel, Virginia "Ginny" Wagenblast, Joanne Widme, Sue Widmer, Barbie Windsor, and Beth Zeko. Thanks to Katie Wolf, Northwest Quilters, Portland, Oregon, for your "Flying Geese" shortcut on page 67. Our thanks, too, to the following Columbia County, Oregon, businesses for their support of *Fresh Air in the Attic*: Fibers & Stitches Quilt Shop, Forever Quilting, and Mustard Seed Quilting.

Our gratitude to Allison LaBarbera and Classic Cottons and for your generosity in providing the quilters with such beautiful fabrics for their creations.

**To purchase any of the featured fabrics,
please contact Classic Cottons at (212) 391-2300
or go online at www.classiccottons.com.**

CONTENTS

LET THE FRESH AIR IN

By Tricia Brown, Editor

Trip Around the World, Log Cabin, Birds in the Air, Crazy Quilt, Rail Fence, Snowball, Nine Patch, Flying Geese, and more. These classic quilt blocks have stood the test of time. But that's no reason why they have to look like they just came out of the attic. With fun patterns and lush, colorful fabrics in the able hands of experienced quilters, the classics have found a new and vibrant look in *Fresh Air in the Attic.*

Many of us have a passion for heirloom quilts, whether they've come to us through family channels, garage sales, or online auctions. Let's see if this describes you: You hit the pause button on a period movie when you spot an old quilt in a scene. You've been known to spend foolishly on misshapen tops that looked far better on e-Bay than they did in person. You'd fondle the fabric at the quilt museum if the docent wasn't giving you the eye. You are a traditionalist—the classic blocks have a special appeal in their geometry and symmetry, in their intriguing names and histories and, often, in the mystery surrounding the identities of their makers.

If you're like me, close examination of a vintage quilt is a trip to a new level of humility. Hand cutting, hand piecing, hand quilting. All with a precision that I can't seem to achieve even with the latest tools! (Forget sliced bread. The rotary cutter was the best invention of the twentieth century.) Fortunately, we can be traditionalists without being purists. Today's quilters can design with computer programs; see-through rulers and self-healing cutting mats are the norm; and making perfectly proportioned triangles is a cinch. So creating an "out-of-the-attic classic" has never been easier.

The seven beautiful quilts that you'll find in *Fresh Air in the Attic* (eight, counting a miniature of the Log Cabin) were designed, pieced, and quilted by members of the Columbia River Piecemakers Quilt Guild and their friends, a group of country quilters from Columbia County, Oregon. They offer step-by-step instructions, with patterns for all levels, from beginner to experienced. Now it's up to you to choose the design and the color scheme that stirs something in you. Then get busy.

In spring, who can resist the urge to throw open the windows and let that fresh air flow into our stale homes? We invite you to do the same for your creative imagination. Open the attic windows of your mind. Give the classics a shot of fresh air while nourishing the traditionalist in you.

Yes, there is the Patchwork Quilt!

looking to the uninterested observer

like a miscellaneous collection of

odd bits and ends of calico,

but to me it is a precious reliquary

of past treasures . . .

—ANNETTE (PSEUD.),
"THE PATCHWORK QUILT," 1845

GENERAL INSTRUCTIONS

Your Work Space

I dream of a spacious, well-lit sewing room with plenty of shelving, a pool-table-sized work surface and an ironing board that's as long and wide as an executive desk. The right height sewing surface; the ergonomically correct chair. Then reality sets in. My sewing room doubles as a small guest room, so my squeaky chair backs up into a twin bed, which is good for laying out blocks for a twin-sized quilt, but nothing bigger. My stash is in clear plastic bins, and the ironing board has to be moved to close the door. Well, at least I can close the door. I used to pack and unpack my materials at the dining room table each time I sat down to sew. Hey, I turned out a couple of very nice quilts at that table . . . even if my family did have to eat on their laps.

Innovative quilters share space-saving tips, like hanging a flannel-backed tablecloth on the wall, flannel side out. Fabric adheres nicely to the flannel, and you can easily play with block designs. A corkboard is good for pinning up your ideas, too.

Place your iron and ironing board nearby, maybe even waist-high, a twist away from your seat at the sewing machine. A desktop ironing board with a mini iron is terrific for quick pressing on a small platform.

Invest in your lighting. It'll save your eyes and improve your color judgment. I have a gooseneck lamp and a moveable-arm light to keep my head from casting shadows.

Make sure your sewing machine is clean, oiled, and in good working condition. A mid-quilt breakdown can result in a quilter's meltdown. Set your stitch length at 10 to 12 stitches per inch. A size 80 needle will do the job; replace it with each new quilt, so it's good and sharp.

What else should you have nearby? A cutting mat and see-through rulers (big and small), rotary cutter and a stash of fresh blades, seam ripper, pins, scissors. A supply of freezer paper or fusible web for appliqué, a notebook and pencil, graph paper, bias tape maker, tape measure, yardstick, masking tape. All of these are handy. I like the magnetic-style pin holder. Plastic sandwich bags or freezer bags are perfect, portable storage units for organizing as you cut small pieces.

Some quilters get more done with a radio on; others prepare for a new quilt project by stocking up on chick flicks for their sewing room "theater." Do what works for you.

Lastly, don't work in a vacuum. Join a circle of quilters and exchange ideas for new tools and shortcuts at meetings and retreats.

Thread

Spend on your thread—buy the best 100% cotton available and have plenty on hand. If your quilt is mostly light-colored, go with light thread; no darker than the darkest value. When in doubt, choose a neutral tan or medium gray. Don't run quilting thread through the machine. The coated surface just doesn't work well.

Fabric

Prewash and iron your fabric . . . or not. You'll find quilters in each camp. Washed fabric is more limp, but if the colors are going to run, better you should know before it's sewn into place next to a light fabric. Some quilters hit their fabric with a little sizing or spray starch on the ironing board to firm it up slightly. If you don't wash the fabric, choose a batting that will shrink slightly, along with the quilt top and backing, when the quilt is washed.

Cutting

Behold the rotary cutter and self-healing mat, your best friends. The first cut you make is to align the two selvage edges and cut them off. Yes, there are lines on the mat to help you square up the fabric and make cuts, but more experienced quilters say that mats can distort with age and use. For precision cutting, they only trust the guidelines on their see-through rulers.

Save time by stacking up to 4 layers of fabric and make a clean cut with a fresh blade. Also, be sure to close the blade after each cut to prevent any accidents.

Chain-piecing

Here's a great shortcut for the repetitive sewing in nearly every quilt design. For example, to sew 24 pieces of Unit A to 24 pieces of Unit B, run them through your machine one after another with a short chain of thread linking them. Cut apart and press after you've completed that stage. It saves time and thread because you're not pulling out a tail and clipping after each piece.

Pressing and Pinning

And you thought your days at the ironing board were over when they invented Perma Press clothes. Use your iron after each sewing step and you will be rewarded with uniform blocks and a precision-made quilt top. The general rule of thumb is to press both edges of a seam toward the darker of the two fabrics. Remember, to avoid any distortions, press and lift without sliding the iron side to side or pulling on the fabric. Also, pay attention to pressing directions in quilt patterns, as the general rule may be broken to avoid bunching up too much fabric in one corner seam. If seams are pressed correctly, one row to the left, the next to the right, when they are joined, the corners will interlock beautifully.

We suggest you use pins liberally to secure placement of seams and points. We've found that there are pinners and there are PINNERS. The fanatic may be the last one to finish at the quilt retreat, but when that quilt top floats to the ground for viewing, it's as flat as a top sheet. Others look like a topographic map of the Rockies.

Top Assembly

Traditionally, quilts come together in horizontal rows that are joined to each other until an entire top is completed. Then it's time to add one or more borders.

But if those square blocks were turned slightly so they form a diamond shape, the quilt is assembled "on point," as is our "Feathered Frenzy" quilt on page 43. This is not something you decide when it's time to lay out your quilt. Normally it's part of the plan from the beginning, since you'll be building the quilt from one corner to the opposite corner in diagonal rows. Half-square triangles along the edges are included in the design to fill the gaps and make all four sides straight. Check out the Feathered Frenzy directions for more on this dynamic method.

Borders

To add one or more borders, follow these steps: Sew a fabric strip on the left and then the right sides. Trim off the excess fabric, making sure the corners are nice and square. Then join the top and bottom border strips, trim off the excess fabric, and square off the corners. Repeat for additional borders.

For those who like a little variety, consider a mitered corner instead, so that the seam runs diagonally from the corner of the border to the corner of the quilt body, like a picture frame. The designers of our "Wild Blue Yonder" rail-fence quilt chose to make a mitered border and were raving about a new tool they've discovered. Learn more about it on page 21.

And what is life? A crazy quilt

Sorrow and joy, and grace and guilt

With here and there a square of blue

For some old happiness we know;

And so the hand of time will take

The fragments of our lives and make

Out of life's remnants, as they fall,

A thing of beauty, after all.

— DOUGLAS MALLOCH
[1877–1938]

CRAZY QUILT

GONE CRAZY

RATING: *Beginner. It's hard to go wrong with these simple directions.*

CLASSIC BLOCK: CRASY QUILT

DESIGNED AND TIED BY CATHY LUNDBERG

PIECED AND EMBELLISHED BY CATHY LUNDBERG, BETH ZEKO, AND CHRIS STANSBURY

The Crazy Quilt has been an enduring favorite since it reached its peak of popularity in the Victorian era. This form of scrap quilt uses up bits and pieces of fabric that do not conform to specific shapes. The pictured quilt top was made with 12" finished blocks using 30 different fabrics. Following are directions for a simpler configuration that can be repeated and rotated to make a wall hanging. This will familiarize you with the technique that can be used with any number of fabrics and any size block to make as large a quilt as you desire. Use the cutting template to speed your progress. Add special embellishments such as embroidery, beads, lace, and buttons to make your Crazy Quilt as simple or complex as you like.

Finished block size: 6" x 6"
Finished quilt size: 48" x 48"

Fabric Requirements
16 fat quarters (or 32—for twice the variety)
3 ½ yards for backing and binding
100% cotton embroidery or tatting thread in various colors
Batting

Cutting Directions
1. Cut all 16 fat quarters into fourths, making (64) 9" squares. If you are using 32 fat quarters, cut (2) 9" squares from each (for a total of 64 squares).

2. Divide the 64 squares into 16 stacks of 4. Make 16 photocopies of the template on page 17 and pin on the top layer of each stack.

3. Use your rotary cutter to cut along the solid lines, then note the number for that piece and store in numbered plastic bags.

4. Repeat number 3 until all of the stacks are cut.

Sewing Directions

Note: As you assemble your squares, you may randomly choose any piece from the appropriate bag. Check template for placement of each new piece. All seams are $\frac{1}{4}$".

1. Following template design, sew pieces 1 and 2, right sides together, with a $\frac{1}{4}$" seam. Press open.

2. Lay piece 3, right sides together, on piece 1 (check template for placement). Sew along the edge. Press open.

3. Sew pieces 4 and 5 together and press open. Referring to the template, align sewn piece 4-5 with piece 1-2-3. You may find it helpful to straighten the edge of 4-5 to make alignment easier. Sew and press as before.

4. Seam pieces 6 and 7 together and press open. Straighten edge, if desired, and join to 1-2-3-4-5 piece.

5. Lastly, sew piece 8 to complete the block. Press open.

6. Trim to unfinished block of $6\frac{1}{2}$".

7. Decorate the seams, if desired, by hand or by machine. But do not embellish all the way to the edge, because you'll lose $\frac{1}{4}$" all around the block when the blocks are sewn together.

8. Repeat steps and make 64 blocks, then arrange into 8 rows of 8 blocks each.

9. Embellish seams between blocks using 8 or more different colors of 100% cotton embroidery or tatting thread.

Backing and Binding

Sandwich the top, batting, and backing. Using two strands of embroidery thread, tie the quilt by making a French knot in the center of each square. To begin each knot, leave a 2" thread tail as you go from the back to the front of the quilt. Likewise, as you complete the knot, leave another 2" tail at the back. Tie these four strands together in a secure square knot, and leave sufficient thread to allow for any future re-tying.

Use double bias binding to finish the edges.

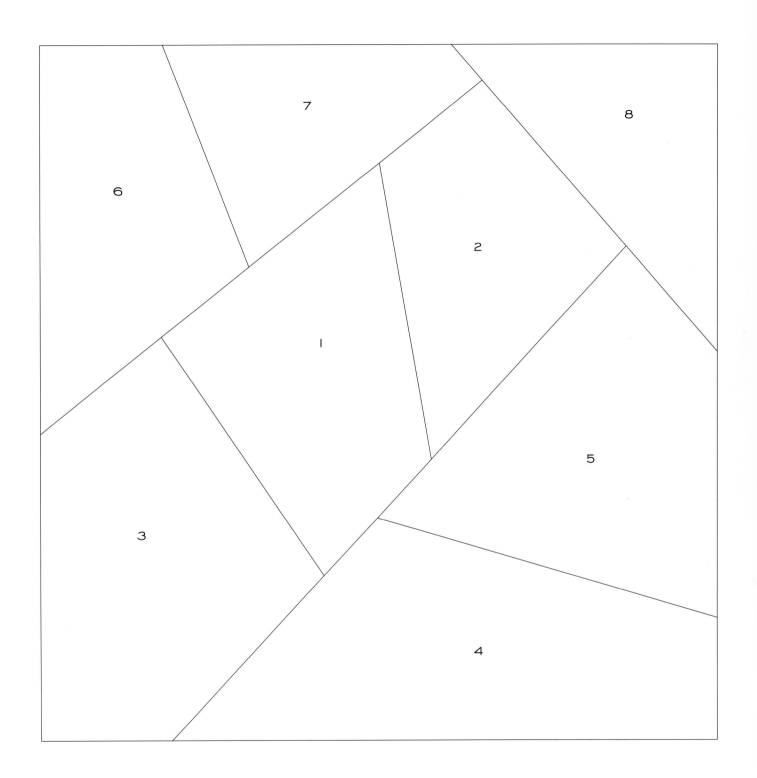

MAKE 16 COPIES OF THIS TEMPLATE AT 100%. USE EACH TEMPLATE AS YOUR GUIDE FOR CUTTING THROUGH 4 LAYERS OF FAT QUARTERS.

Home to my poor wife,

who works all day like a horse,

at the making of her hangings

for our chamber and bed.

— THE DIARY OF SAMUEL PEPYS
[1633–1703]

RAIL FENCE

WILD BLUE YONDER

RATING: *A fun project for beginners*

CLASSIC BLOCK: RAIL FENCE

DESIGNED AND PIECED BY DONNA ADAMS, KATHIE HARRIS, AND SUE WIDMER

QUILTED BY PAM AND RAY ADAMS, MUSTARD SEED QUILTING, SCAPPOOSE, OREGON

Like many traditional blocks, the Rail Fence harkens back to the days of frontier America, when what we now know as the Midwest was considered "the West." Also known as Basket Weave, this is one of those patterns with a name that, for the pioneer quilters, reflected an aspect of everyday life. Even today, once you've looked closely at a basket or viewed a split-rail fence zigzagging across a pasture, there's no doubt why those names stuck to this old favorite. In our modernized version, long-arm quilting in a bright yellow thread adds the whimsy of butterflies to the repetitiveness of the five-rail blocks with contrasting borders.

Finished block size: 7 1/2" x 7 1/2"
Finished quilt size: 60" x 75"

Fabric Requirements (Yardage is based on 42" wide fabric)

Fabric 1   3/4 yard No. 7083-2 - Style 3416 Luminaries
Fabric 2   3/4 yard No. 7082-2 - Style 3416 Luminaries
Fabric 3   3/4 yard No. 7081-2 - Style 3416 Luminaries
Fabric 4   3/4 yard No. 7080-2 - Style 3416 Luminaries
Fabric 5   3/4 yard No. 7079-2 - Style 3416 Luminaries
Fabric 6   1/2 yard No. 7080-5 - Style 3416 Luminaries
Fabric 7   7 yards No. 5216-22 - Style 3089 Classic Cotton Calicos
Batting

Cutting Directions

The rail fence blocks are made using Fabrics 1 through 5. Cut each of the five fabrics into (10) 2" strips.

To make the inner border, cut Fabric 6 into 2" strips cutting across the width of the fabric.

For the outer border, cut Fabric 7 down the length of the fabric parallel to the selvage at 6½"–wide strips. You will need four strips that measure 6½" by 2¼ yards.

Remaining portions of Fabric 7 will be used for backing and binding.

Sewing Directions

1. Begin by sewing a strip of Fabric 1 to a strip of Fabric 2, right sides together, along the length of the strips. Press toward Fabric 2.

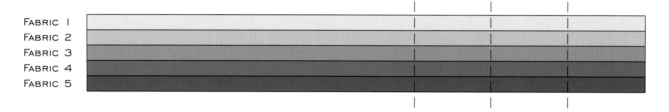

2. Sew a strip of Fabric 3 to Fabric 2 edge, right sides together, along the long edge. Press toward Fabric 3.

3. Continue in the same fashion, adding Fabric 4, and press toward Fabric 4.

4. Sew Fabric 5 to strip set and press toward Fabric 5. Set aside.

5. Repeat these steps until you have 10 of these strip sets.

6. Now cut each of the strip sets into 8" squares. You get should 5 of these squares from each strip set. You will need 48 of these blocks to assemble the quilt top, leaving you with two extra blocks.

Top Assembly

1. Begin by setting out your blocks in rows following the diagram for Row 1, then sewing them together. Press seams that join the blocks all in the same direction. Make 4 sets of Row 1.

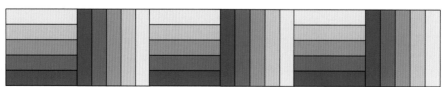

Row 1

2. Repeat following the diagram for Row 2. Make 4 sets of Row 2. Press in the opposite direction of Row 1.

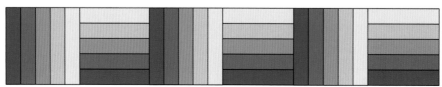

Row 2

3. Lay out the rows, alternating Row 1 and Row 2, then sew the rows together to form the quilt top.

4. Take the Fabric 6 strips that you cut for the inner border and sew them together into one long strip using a bias seam to reduce bulk.

5. Sew the strip of Fabric 6 to one side of each of the four outer border strips from Fabric 7, cutting as needed. Press toward the outer border.

6. Sew these border strips to all four edges of the quilt, starting and stopping $1/4$" from each edge. Miter the corners using your favorite method, or try Marti Michell's My Favorite Mitering Ruler.

Backing, Quilting, and Binding

Sew your backing to allow about 4"–6" of extra fabric beyond the finished size. Likewise, your batting should extend beyond the finished top. Layer with batting and top, baste, and quilt as desired. Trim edges and bind.

Blessed are the children of quilters,

for they shall inherit

the quilts.

— ANONYMOUS

TRIP AROUND THE WORLD

TRIP AROUND THE COUNTY

RATING: *Intermediate. Once you get past the cutting, it's a breeze!*

CLASSIC BLOCK: TRIP AROUND THE WORLD
DESIGNED BY KAY LOCKWOOD
PIECED BY KAY LOCKWOOD AND JOYCE BECKMAN
QUILTED BY PAM AND RAY ADAMS, MUSTARD SEED QUILTING, SCAPPOOSE, OREGON

Trip Around the World quilts were among those used to wordlessly direct escaping slaves on the Underground Railroad in the 1800s. The appearance and position of certain quilts at homes along the way spoke to the travelers of direction, distance, and safety. Trip Around the World rose to its height of popularity during the 1930s, but remains a hit today. It's a fast and fun scrap quilt set in a diamond pattern that progresses from light to dark and back again. As Sunshine and Shadow, the pattern was also a favorite among the Amish quilters of Lancaster County, Pennsylvania.

Finished block size: $2\frac{1}{2}$" x $2\frac{1}{2}$"
Finished quilt size: 43" x 53"

Fabric Requirements (Yardage is based on 42" wide fabric)

Fabric 1	Light	$\frac{3}{4}$ yard No. 5322-91T - Style 3089 Classic Cotton Florals
Fabric 2	Medium Light Print	$\frac{3}{4}$ yard No. 7082-1 - Style 3416 Luminaries
Fabric 3	Medium Print	$2\frac{3}{4}$ yards No. 5215-20T - Style 3089 Classic Cotton Florals (includes backing)
Fabric 4	Medium Dark	$\frac{3}{4}$ yard No. 7082-2 - Style 3416 Luminaries
Fabric 5	Dark	$1\frac{1}{4}$ yards No. 7081-5 - Style 3416 Luminaries (includes binding)
Batting		

Cutting Instructions

Cut (7) 3-inch strips of each of the 5 fabrics, then sub-cut the following. Cut your longest strips first—you can cut shorter strips from the unused ends. To stay organized, as you cut the strips, place them in stacks and label them with Fabric number and length.

From Fabric 1 strips, cut:
(2) 42" strips
(4) 24" strips
(2) 12" strips
(4) 9" strips
(4) 3" squares

From Fabric 2 strips, cut:
(2) 48" strips
(4) 21" strips
(2) 18" strips
(4) 5" strips
(4) 3" squares

From Fabric 3 strips, cut:
(4) 27" strips
(2) 24" strips
(4) 18" strips
(4) 3" squares

From Fabric 4 strips, cut:
(2) 30" strips
(4) 27" strips
(4) 15" strips
(5) 3" squares

From Fabric 5 strips, cut:
(2) 36" strips
(4) 27" strips
(4) 12" strips
(2) 5" strips
(4) 3" squares

Sewing Directions

1. Join the strips by row in the order shown in the diagram. You will be making two identical sections, A and B.

2. For Rows 1 and 2, take (1) 5" strip of Fabric 5 and place, right sides together, with (1) 12" strip of Fabric 1. Align the centers by folding the strips in half and marking the center on the right side with an erasable marker. Join with a $\frac{1}{4}$" seam, then press in the direction of Fabric 5.

3. For Row 3, take (1) 18" strip of Fabric 2, fold in half and mark the center, place right sides together, and join to Row 2. Press in the direction of Fabric 2. For Row 4 use the 24" strip of Fabric 3. For Row 5, use the 30" strip of Fabric 4. For Row 6, use the 36" strip of Fabric 5. Continue to build up to Row 8,

aligning each new strip with the row above it at center, placing right sides together, then joining with a ¼" seam allowance. Press each new seam in the opposite direction as you did on the previous seam.

4. At Row 9, allow a 1" gap at center between the left and right ends of the Section A assembly (see Diagram A). For Row 10, make that center gap 7". For Row 11, make that center gap 13".

5. For the remaining rows, don't build from the center, but rather align each new strip with the far right and far left edges. Continue to press each new seam in the opposite direction as the last.

6. When Section A is completed, cut into 3" vertical strips beginning at center. Using your center line as a guide, measure 1½" on each side and cut a 3" strip. Be precise in your cutting. Although there is room for adjustment, precision is important. Continue cutting 3" strips, moving away from center, for a total of 21 strips. As you cut, realign the strips, sliding them up or down on your cutting surface so they form a rectangle—the shape that they'll be when they are sewn together. See Diagram B.

To keep the strips organized, have a big safety pin handy, and starting from your left, put the top end of each strip on the pin in a stacking order that will make sense to you when you're ready to sew them together.

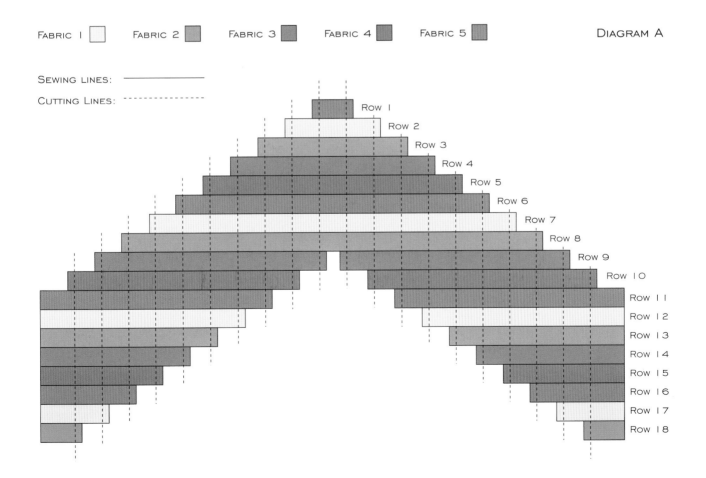

FABRIC 1 ▢ FABRIC 2 ▨ FABRIC 3 ▨ FABRIC 4 ▨ FABRIC 5 ▨   DIAGRAM A

SEWING LINES: ————
CUTTING LINES: - - - - - - -

Row 1
Row 2
Row 3
Row 4
Row 5
Row 6
Row 7
Row 8
Row 9
Row 10
Row 11
Row 12
Row 13
Row 14
Row 15
Row 16
Row 17
Row 18

7. Join the strips to form a rectangle, and press all new seams in the same direction.

PRESSING DIRECTION ⟶   CENTER

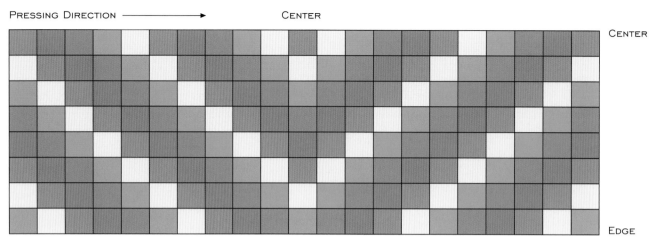

CENTER

EDGE

DIAGRAM B—SECTIONS A & B

8. Repeat all of the above steps to make Section B, then cut it into the vertical strips and join them to make a rectangular block as shown in Diagram B. Press all new seams in the same direction as you did with Section A.

9. Next, using the 3" blocks that you've already cut, make a single strip that will connect Section A with Section B. It will look like this:

⟵   PRESS IN OPPOSITE DIRECTION
OF SECTIONS A AND B   CENTER

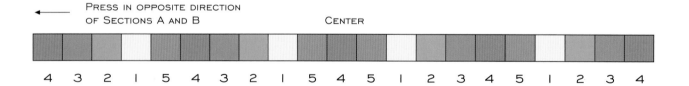

4   3   2   1   5   4   3   2   1   5   4   5   1   2   3   4   5   1   2   3   4

DIAGRAM C

10. Press the seams in this connecting strip in the opposite direction as you did for Sections A and B.

11. Join Sections A and B to each side of the connecting strip to create a diamond shape at the center of the quilt. If you like, you can make a larger quilt by adding one or more borders before you layer and quilt.

Backing, Quilting, and Binding

For a single-print backing, use 2 yards of Fabric 3. Since the fabric is 42" wide, you'll have to seam pieces of the fabric into a center band to allow enough backing to extend beyond the edges of the top while you are quilting. Or, as long as you have to add a band, consider using scraps from a favorite second color and create a contrasting color band across the back.

Layer and quilt using your favorite method. Bind with Fabric 5.

How much piecin' a quilt is like livin' a life!

You can give the same kind of pieces

to two persons, and one will make a

"nine-patch" and one'll make a

"wild goose chase,"

and there will be two quilts

made out of the same kind of pieces,

and jest as different as they can be.

And that is jest the way with livin'.

— AUNT JANE PARISH
CAROLINE OBENCHAIN (ELIZA CALVERT HALL, PSEUD.)
"AUNT JANE OF KENTUCKY," 1907

SNOWBALL AND NINE-PATCH

SHADOW CATS

RATING: *The appliquéd cats bump up this Beginner quilt to an Intermediate level.*

CLASSIC BLOCKS: SNOWBALL AND NINE-PATCH
DESIGNED AND PIECED BY KATIE GARMAN; APPLIQUÉ CATS BY NIKKI DAVIS
QUILTED BY PAM AND RAY ADAMS, MUSTARD SEED QUILTING, SCAPPOOSE, OREGON

The Nine-Patch block is a golden oldie, found in pioneer quilts as early as 1800. By combining this versatile traditional block with the more contemporary Snowball, a beautiful curved pattern emerges, not nearly as difficult to make as it looks. Now appliqué your quilt with playful kittens that threaten to claw their way onto the bed. Make them as "shadowy" as you like, with their dark shapes blending into your darker fabric. To allow the cats to stand out more, choose cat fabric with greater contrast against the quilt top. Another option is to make fewer blocks and add a third border color for your kitties to better show against their playground.

Finished block size: 6" x 6"
Finished quilt size: 90" x 102"

Fabric Requirements (Yardage is based on 42" wide fabric)

Fabric 1 6$\frac{1}{2}$ yards light fabric for background
Fabric 2 5$\frac{1}{2}$ yards of darker contrasting fabric
Fabric 3 1 yard black fabric for cat appliqués
9 yards (suggest Fabric 2) for backing and binding
Batting

Cutting Directions

Cut (32) 2$\frac{1}{2}$" strips from Fabric 1
Cut (22) 6$\frac{1}{2}$" strips from Fabric 1; sub-cut into (127) 6$\frac{1}{2}$" squares
Cut (72) 2$\frac{1}{2}$" strips from Fabric 2; sub-cut 32 of the strips into (508) 2$\frac{1}{2}$" squares

Sewing Directions
Nine-Patch:

Using 16 strips of Fabric 1 and 8 strips of Fabric 2, sew the length of the strips as shown to make 8 strip sets of Unit A. Press toward darker fabric. Sub-cut into (128) 2$\frac{1}{2}$" strips.

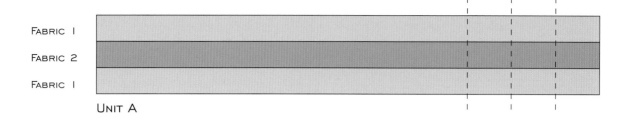

FABRIC 1

FABRIC 2

FABRIC 1

UNIT A

Using 16 strips of Fabric 1 and 32 strips of Fabric 2, sew the length of the strips as shown to make 16 strip sets of Unit B. Press toward darker fabric. Sub-cut into (256) 2½" strips:

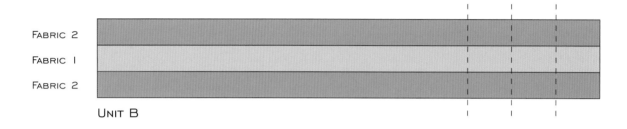

FABRIC 2

FABRIC 1

FABRIC 2

UNIT B

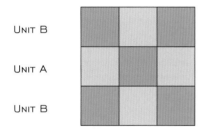

UNIT B

UNIT A

UNIT B

Sew together as shown to make (128) Nine-Patch blocks.

Snowball Block:

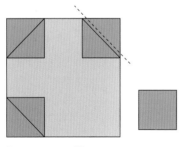

SNOWBALL BLOCK

There are several methods for making the standard Snowball block. Pam Bono's The Angler© was the favorite of our designer. But if you prefer the traditional route, here's a surefire way of getting your corners right:

Lay out a 6½" block of Fabric 2. Place a 2½" square of Fabric 1 in the corner with the reverse side up. Align the edges on both sides. Draw a diagonal line across the back of Fabric 1 as shown below. Sew on the line. Chain-piece 127 blocks, one corner at a time. Trim off extra fabric ¼" from the seam and press toward the corner.

Top Assembly

Sew nine rows of 15 blocks using (8) Nine-Patches and (7) Snowballs. Press toward Snowballs. See Row 1.

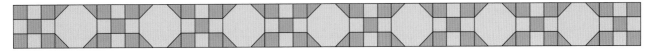

Row 1

Sew eight rows of 15 blocks using (8) Snowballs and (7) Nine-Patches. Press toward Snowballs. See Row 2.

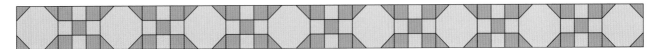

Row 2

Sew 17 rows together, alternating Rows 1 and 2.

Adding the Shadow Cats

Use your favorite appliqué method to include as many mischievous kitties as you like. One standard is to use freezer paper to stabilize your appliqué fabric. These cat templates are printed at a reduced size, so photocopy the page at 225% to get the correct template size. Trace them onto freezer paper and cut out. Lay out the freezer paper shapes, shiny side up, and lay a rough cut section of black fabric over the paper. Using a dry iron, press lightly and the paper will adhere. Cut around the shape about $1/4$" beyond the edge of the freezer paper, then plan where to place the cat shapes. You can remove the freezer paper now and pin the cats into place, or wait until after you've needle-turn appliquéd the shapes. If you choose the latter, eliminate excess fabric bulk behind the cats by cutting through the back of the quilt top, trimming away the piecework behind the appliqué, and peeling away the freezer paper.

Backing, Quilting, and Binding

Sew your backing to allow about 4"–6" inches of extra fabric beyond the finished size of about 90" x 120". Likewise, your batting should extend beyond the finished top. Layer with batting and top, and quilt as desired. Trim edges and bind with Fabric 2.

MAKE SEVERAL COPIES AT 225% OF THE KITTY TEMPLATES AT RIGHT BEFORE TRACING ONTO FREEZER PAPER.

When your work

speaks for itself,

don't interrupt.

— HENRY J. KAISER
[1882–1967]

BIRDS IN THE AIR

FEATHERED FRENZY

RATING: *Intermediate. If you've never tried an "on point" quilt, now's your chance!*

CLASSIC BLOCK: BIRDS IN THE AIR
DESIGNED BY AMANDA MCFERON
PIECED BY AMANDA MCFERON AND LINDA GILCHRIST
LONG-ARM QUILTED BY LORRIE HULSOPPLE

It takes little imagination to see the movement of flight in this vivid beauty. With a name taken from nature, Birds in the Air is a classic block that remains an adaptable favorite. The antique appliquéd bluebird quilt, folded at left, was made by Louise Wilken.

Finished block size: 6" x 6"
Finished quilt size: 66" x 85"

Fabric Requirements (Yardage is based on 42" wide fabric)

Note: For clarity's sake, we'll refer to the pieced triangle units as "Birds" and the various colored, un-pieced triangle units as "Nests."

For Birds:
Fabric A   2 yards Dark Purple No. 2968-30M Cracked Ice
Fabric B   1 yard Blue No. 5963-2 - Style 3296 Gemstones

For Nests and border squares:
Fabric C   1 yard Yellow No. 6386-42T - Style 3281 Endless Possibilities
Fabric D   1 yard Rose No. 5963-14 - Style 3296 Gemstones
Fabric E   ³/₄ yard Salmon No. 5594-74T - Style 3171 Muted Moments
Fabric F   ³/₄ yard Light Purple No. 5387-35T - Style 3296 Gemstones
Fabric G   ³/₄ yard Green No. 5592-55T - Style 3171 Muted Moments

For side and corner triangles, borders, and backing:
Fabric H   10 yards Blue No. 7081-2 - Style 3416 Luminaries

Batting

Cutting Directions for Top (not including borders)

Note: Cut strips across the width of fabric.

Fabric A   Cut (8) 6" strips, then sub-cut into (46) 6" squares

Fabric B   Cut (4) 6" strips, then sub-cut into (23) 6" squares

Fabric C   Cut (2) 7½" strips, then sub-cut into (10) 7½" squares

Fabric D   Cut (2) 7½" strips, then sub-cut into (10) 7½" squares

Fabric E   Cut (1) 7½" strip, then sub-cut into (3) 7½" squares

Fabric F   Cut (1) 7½" strip, then sub-cut into (5) 7½" squares

Fabric G   Cut (1) 7½" strips, then sub-cut into (4) 7½" squares

Fabric H   Cut (5) 10½" squares, then sub-cut twice on the diagonal to create 20 large triangles

              Cut (2) 6" squares, then sub-cut once on the diagonal to create 4 small triangles

Sewing Directions

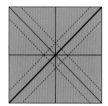

DIAGRAM A

1. Select (23) 6" squares each from Fabrics A and B. On the reverse of each of the lighter squares, draw two diagonal lines from corner to corner, making an X. Then place A and B squares right sides together and stitch a ¼" seam on each side of both lines. Draw two more lines to make the square into four quarters as shown in Diagram A. Cut on all solid lines. Each 6" square will make 8 half-square triangles totaling 184. Open and press toward darker fabric.

DIAGRAM B

2. Sew two half-square triangle sets together (see Diagram B) and press toward darker fabric. Make 59 sets.

3. Take remaining (23) 6" Fabric A squares, stack them in groups of 4, draw corner-to-corner lines, as well as the two additional lines to divide square into quarters. Do not sew these squares, but cut them apart, following lines, into 184 triangles.

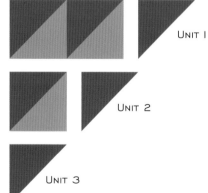

UNIT 1

UNIT 2

UNIT 3

DIAGRAM C

4. Using Diagram C as your guide, sew one of these triangles to each of the half-square triangle sets you made in Step 2. Make 59 of Unit 1.

5. Sew the remaining half-square triangles to a triangle, as shown in Diagram C, and press toward dark. Make 59 of Unit 2.

6. Referring to Diagram C, sew a Unit 1 to the top of a Unit 2, then sew a triangle (Unit 3) to the bottom of Unit 2 to create Bird triangle.

7. Take the (32) 7½" Nest squares, stack them in groups of 3 or 4 and, using your straight edge and rotary cutter, cut them once diagonally, corner to corner. Lay out a Bird triangle and a Nest triangle, right sides together (with wrong side of bird triangle up), and carefully sew a ¼" seam. As you sew, make sure you do

not cut off any triangle points (the bird "beaks") with your seam. You may reduce the seam allowance slightly if needed. Press toward the Nest fabric. See Diagram D.

8. Square all blocks to 6½" (do any necessary trimming on the Nest fabric). The final count should be:

Fabric C   20 blocks   Fabric F   10 blocks
Fabric D   15 blocks   Fabric G   8 blocks
Fabric E   6 blocks

DIAGRAM D

Top Assembly

The quilt top will be assembled on point, in strips, beginning with the upper left corner as Row 1.

1. Refer to Diagram E and lay out blocks in rows to make sure the bird and nest colors are positioned correctly.

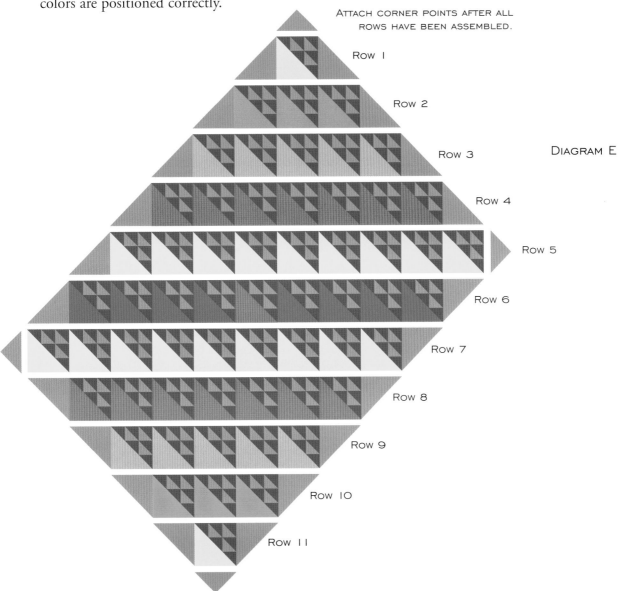

ATTACH CORNER POINTS AFTER ALL ROWS HAVE BEEN ASSEMBLED.

Row 1
Row 2
Row 3
Row 4
Row 5
Row 6
Row 7
Row 8
Row 9
Row 10
Row 11

DIAGRAM E

2. Lay out the large half-square triangles from Fabric H at the ends of each row to create the final rectangle shape of the top. It will help to label the rows by number.

3. For Row 1, sew a larger triangle from Fabric H to each side of the single corner square and press toward the triangles. Trim off any fabric "ears," but do not trim excess fabric from triangle pieces until the top is assembled. See Diagram E.

4. Sew the blocks into rows, adding the triangle pieces at each end. Press each row in the opposite direction as you did the previous row.

5. Join rows, building from Row 1 and moving toward the opposite corner. Some quilters prefer to stop midway, call that first half Section 1, then begin on the opposite corner and work toward the middle to create the second half, Section 2. Then they join the two large sections at center. Do what works best for you.

6. Lastly, sew the small triangle pieces from Fabric H to each of the four corners of the quilt.

7. Square up and trim the quilt top, ensuring that the Bird block points along the outside are at least $1/4$" from the raw edge.

Border Cutting Directions and Assembly

Note: Cut strips across the width of fabric.

Border 1:

From Fabric H, cut (4) 3" strips. Join ends to form one long strip, then cut it into two equal lengths.

Also from Fabric H, cut (3) $3^5/8$" strips. Join ends to form one long strip, then cut it into two equal lengths.

Sew the 3" border strips to the left and right sides of the top, using pins to ensure that the Bird block points will meet the border seam exactly. Press toward border and trim excess fabric. Next attach the $3^5/8$" border strips to the top and bottom. Press toward border. Check corners for square and trim excess fabric.

Border 2:

From Fabric H, cut (5) $5^1/4$" strips, then sub-cut into (33) $5^1/4$" squares. Next cut the squares on the diagonal twice, corner to corner, creating 4 triangles from each square.

From Fabrics C, D, E, F, G, cut (2) 3" strips from each color, then sub-cut all strips into 3" squares.

UNIT 4

Sew a Fabric H triangle to two sides of each 3" square to make Unit 4 as shown in Diagram F. Trim off "ears." Make 70.

DIAGRAM F

Join 19 sets of Unit 4 to create a strip for the left border (see Diagram G). Add a triangle of Fabric H to each end of the border strip. Repeat for right border strip. Square up, making sure to leave ¼" for seam allowance.

DIAGRAM G

Join 16 sets of Unit 4 to create a strip for the top border. Add a triangle of Fabric H to each end. Repeat for bottom border strip. Square up, making sure to leave ¼" for seam allowance.

Attach side borders first, using pins to ensure that points meet the seam exactly. Press toward Border 1. Next attach the top and bottom border strips, matching the diamond points at each corner. Press toward Border 1.

Border 3:

From Fabric H, cut (10) 6½" strips. Join ends to form one long strip. Attach left and right borders first. Press toward Border 3. Trim excess fabric and check corners for square. Finally, attach the top and bottom borders. Press toward Border 3 and ensure that corners are square.

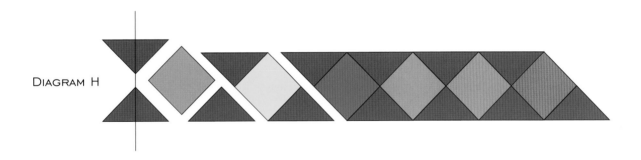

DIAGRAM H

Backing, Quilting, and Binding

Cut backing from Fabric H and seam as necessary, allowing for 4"–6" of fabric extending beyond the quilt top. Layer with batting that also extends beyond the edge of the quilt top. Quilt as desired. Trim, then bind with Fabric A.

I cannot count

my day complete

'til needle, thread,

and fabric meet.

— Anonymous

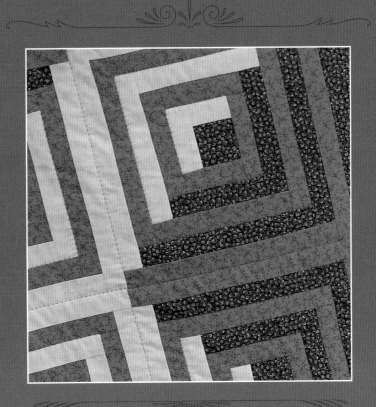

LOG CABIN

BERRY BLUSH

RATING: *Intermediate (mostly because of the center appliqué).*

Otherwise as easy as a berry pie.

CLASSIC BLOCK: LOG CABIN
DESIGN INSPIRED BY AN ANTIQUE LOG CABIN QUILT FROM NEW YORK, CA. 1900
PIECED BY LILY GOODWIN AND TRICIA BROWN
HAND-QUILTED BY LILY GOODWIN, TRICIA BROWN, MARY ANN EMERSON, SUSAN SPAIN,
B. J. CLEVENGER, EVALINE BIXBY, RUTHANNE TARTER, AND EDNA MORSE.

The log cabin is one of the oldest and most versatile of the classic blocks. The center square represents the hearth in the log cabin home and was traditionally a red color. You can control the top's visual effect by choosing a dramatic three-color scheme, or going for a scrappy look using fabrics with softer, graduated values. Rotating the blocks during trial layout sessions shows how the same set of blocks can be rearranged into widely different designs. You can make pinwheels, streaks of lightning or, as shown in this photo, create diamond patterns using a barn-raising-style layout. Reduce the quilt to Queen or Full size by cutting narrower strips or by reducing the number of strips per block. Experiment with paper piecing to make a small quilt like "Little Purple Logs," shown on page 59.

Finished block size: 12"
Finished quilt size: 96" x 120"

Fabric Requirements (Yardage is based on 43" wide fabric)

Light	3 yards No. 5751-31T - Style 3171 Muted Moments
Medium Light	2¼ yards No. 5593-33T - Style 3171 Muted Moments
Medium	7½ yards No. 5594-34T - Style 3171 Muted Moments
Medium Dark	12½ yards No. 5698M-3 - Style 3089
	Classic Cotton Floral (includes backing)
Darkest	3 yards No. 7079-3 - Style 3416
	Luminaries (includes binding)

Cutting Instructions

Cut the 1½" strips across the width of fabric. *Tip:* For the sub-cuts, cut the longest segments first and then cut shorter pieces from the scraps.

Log Cabin Blocks:

Light   Cut (57) $1\frac{1}{2}$" strips, then sub-cut into the following:
(52) $11\frac{1}{2}$" strips
(52) $10\frac{1}{2}$" strips
(52) $7\frac{1}{2}$" strips
(52) $6\frac{1}{2}$" strips
(52) $3\frac{1}{2}$" strips
(52) $2\frac{1}{2}$" strips

Medium Light   Cut (51) $1\frac{1}{2}$" strips, then sub-cut into the following:
(24) $11\frac{1}{2}$" strips
(24) $10\frac{1}{2}$" strips
(24) $9\frac{1}{2}$" strips
(24) $8\frac{1}{2}$" strips
(24) $7\frac{1}{2}$" strips
(24) $6\frac{1}{2}$" strips
(24) $5\frac{1}{2}$" strips
(24) $4\frac{1}{2}$" strips
(24) $3\frac{1}{2}$" strips
(24) $2\frac{1}{2}$" strips

Medium   Cut (147) $1\frac{1}{2}$" strips, then sub-cut into the following:
(76) $12\frac{1}{2}$" strips
(76) $11\frac{1}{2}$" strips
(52) $9\frac{1}{2}$" strips
(128) $8\frac{1}{2}$" strips
(76) $7\frac{1}{2}$" strips
(52) $5\frac{1}{2}$" strips
(128) $4\frac{1}{2}$" strips
(76) $3\frac{1}{2}$" strips

Medium Dark   Cut (3) $2\frac{1}{2}$" strips, then sub-cut into (36) $2\frac{1}{2}$" squares
Cut (30) $1\frac{1}{2}$" strips, then sub-cut into the following:
(36) $10\frac{1}{2}$" strips
(36) $9\frac{1}{2}$" strips
(36) $6\frac{1}{2}$" strips
(36) $5\frac{1}{2}$" strips

Darkest   Cut (4) $2\frac{1}{2}$" strips, then cut into (40) $2\frac{1}{2}$" squares
Cut (35) $1\frac{1}{2}$" strips, then sub-cut into the following:
(40) $10\frac{1}{2}$" strips
(40) $9\frac{1}{2}$" strips
(40) $6\frac{1}{2}$" strips
(40) $5\frac{1}{2}$" strips

CENTERPIECE FOUR-PATCH AND FAN

Medium	Cut (2) 2" strips, then cut into (12) 2" x 7" rectangles
	Cut (2) 12 1/2" squares
Medium Dark	Cut (2) 2" strips, then cut into (12) 2" x 7" rectangles
	Cut (2) 12 1/2" squares
Light	Cut (4) 2" strips, then cut into (24) 2" x 7" rectangles

Sewing Directions

Match steps to the numbers on the diagram. It is extra important to stay square as you build these blocks. Press after adding each "log" and check often to make sure you are staying square. The unfinished block will measure 12 1/2" square.

BLOCK A (Make 32)

BLOCK A

1. Begin with 2 1/2" square of Darkest fabric for center square or "hearth."
2. Join 1 1/2" x 2 1/2" Light fabric to center square. Place right sides together and sew with 1/4" seam allowance. Chain piece 32 units. Cut apart and press open.
3. Adding "logs" in a counter-clockwise movement, chain piece a 1 1/2" x 3 1/2" Light strip to the left side of the block, forming an upside-down L shape with the Light fabric. Repeat for all 32 units. Cut apart and press after each subsequent step. And don't forget to check for square, so you can make adjustments early.
4. Chain piece 1 1/2" x 3 1/2" Medium strip to bottom of each block. Cut apart and press for this and all additional steps.
5. Add 1 1/2" x 4 1/2" Medium strip to right side of each block.
6. Add 1 1/2" x 4 1/2" Medium strip to top of each block.
7. Add 1 1/2" x 5 1/2" Medium strip to left side of each block.
8. Add 1 1/2" x 5 1/2" Darkest strip to bottom of each block.
9. Add 1 1/2" x 6 1/2" Darkest strip to right side of each block.
10. Add 1 1/2" x 6 1/2" Light strip to top of each block.
11. Add 1 1/2" x 7 1/2" Light strip to left side of each block.
12. Add 1 1/2" x 7 1/2" Medium strip to bottom of each block.
13. Add 1 1/2" x 8 1/2" Medium strip to right side of each block.
14. Add 1 1/2" x 8 1/2" Medium strip to top side of each block.
15. Add 1 1/2" x 9 1/2" Medium strip to left side of each block.
16. Add 1 1/2" x 9 1/2" Darkest strip to bottom of each block.
17. Add 1 1/2" x 10 1/2" Darkest strip to right side of each block.
18. Add 1 1/2" x 10 1/2" Light strip to top of each block.
19. Add 1 1/2" x 11 1/2" Light strip to left side of each block.

20. Add 1½" x 11½" Medium strip to bottom of each block.

21. Add 1½" x 12½" Medium strip to right side of each block.

Set aside those 32 units of Block A.

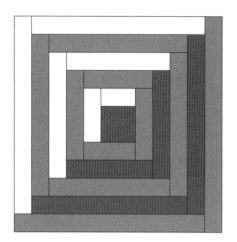

BLOCK B

BLOCK B (Make 20)

Next, following the same instructions, make 20 more blocks, but substitute Medium Dark fabric wherever the above directions indicate Darkest fabric, in Steps 1, 8, 9, 16, and 17.

Set aside those 20 units of Block B.

BLOCK C (Make 8)

Now make 8 blocks using the same steps, but substitute Medium Light fabric in Steps number 2 and 3, 6 and 7, 10 and 11, 14 and 15, 18 and 19.

Use the Darkest fabric for Steps 1, 8, 9, 16, and 17.

One side of the finished block will be all one color—Medium Light—and the other should look like the dark side of your first set of blocks.

Set aside the 8 units of Block C.

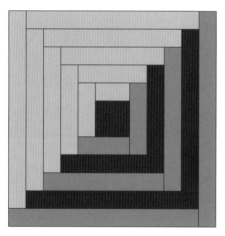

BLOCK C

BLOCK D (Make 16)

These 16 units will be identical to Block C, however, use Medium Dark fabric for Steps 1, 8, 9, 16, and 17.

One side of the finished block will be all Medium Light, and the other should look like the medium dark side of Block B.

Set aside the 16 units of Block D.

BLOCK E
CENTERPIECE FOUR-PATCH AND CIRCLE FAN

1. Gather the (12) 2" strips of Medium, (12) 2" strips of Medium Dark Fabric, plus (24) strips of Light fabric that will form the circle. Gather the (2) 12½" Medium Dark squares and (2) 12½" Medium squares for the four-patch behind the circle.

2. Photocopy the template on page 56 and cut a cardboard, freezer paper, or plastic template as your guide for creating the appliquéd centerpiece. Or use a fusible web product such as Steam-A-Seam. The template includes the ¼" seam allowance.

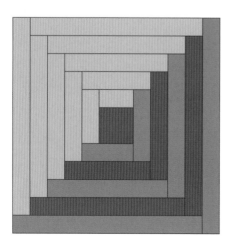

BLOCK D

3. Cut all strips using the template.

4. Lay out four $12\frac{1}{2}$" squares with Medium Dark in upper left corner, Medium in upper right; Medium in lower left; and Medium Dark in lower right. Overlap the raw edges to emulate the $\frac{1}{4}$" seam allowance, but *do not* sew the four squares together.

5. Lightly mark two circles centered on the four-patch layout representing the inner and outer edges of the fan circle. One should measure 9" across and the other 22" inches across. You may make the circles from cardboard or plastic, or try a fabric compass. These lines will guide your appliqué stitches. Accuracy will be essential when the squares and circles are joined.

6. Lay out strips in alternating bars on each of the four squares. Use alternating Light and Medium Dark strips on the Medium fabric, and alternating Light and Medium strips on the Medium Dark squares.

7. Sew the long sides of the strips together with a $\frac{1}{4}$" seam allowance, working one-quarter of the circle at a time. When finished, the strips should measure $1\frac{3}{8}$" at the top, and a fat $\frac{1}{2}$" at the bottom.

8. Pin into place on the appropriate square and needle-turn appliqué the top and bottom edges of the one-quarter circle, making sure that the circles will align when the blocks are joined.

9. Repeat for each square. *Do not join the blocks* until it's time to piece the entire top.

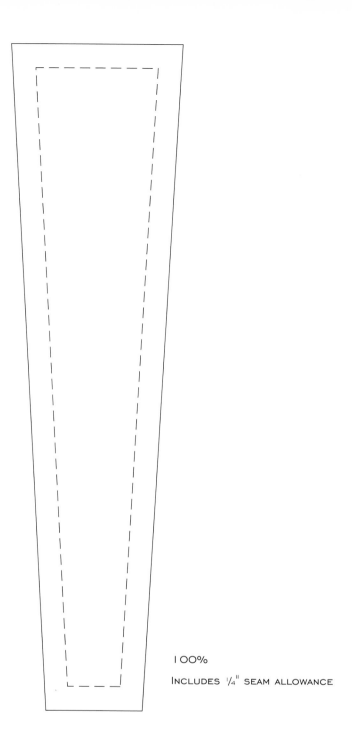

100%

INCLUDES ¼" SEAM ALLOWANCE

Assembling the Top

Sew 10 rows of 8 blocks each, rotating the blocks to create the barn-raising effect as shown in Diagram A.

As you join the blocks into rows, press the new seams for each row in the same direction. Press the next row of seams in the opposite direction. By alternating directions on each subsequent row, the corners should fit snugly together as you join row to row.

Blocks

Row 1	D	C	D	A	A	D	C	D
Row 2	C	D	A	A	A	A	D	C
Row 3	D	A	A	B	B	A	A	D
Row 4	A	A	B	B	B	B	A	A
Row 5	A	B	B	E	E	B	B	A
Row 6	A	B	B	E	E	B	B	A
Row 7	A	A	B	B	B	B	A	A
Row 8	D	A	A	B	B	A	A	D
Row 9	C	D	A	A	A	A	D	C
Row 10	D	C	D	A	A	D	C	D

Backing, Quilting, and Binding

Since this is a king-sized quilt, the backing will need two seams. You can divide it into even thirds, or use the width of fabric for the middle panel and trim only the left and right panels. As usual, cut the backing and batting 4"–6" longer and wider than the quilt top.

For this sample, the team of quilters worked together to stitch in the ditch on every other "log" and around each hearth. They selected this method because, with so many quilters, varying stitch lengths might detract from the beauty of the quilt if they were more visible. For the center panel, the women quilted around each piece of the fan, and one quilter used a template to create a special pattern in each corner of the four-patch block behind the circle fan.

To draw more attention to your hand-quilting, choose a lighter color for the backing, or pick a thread with greater contrast against the backing fabric.

DIAGRAM A

LITTLE PURPLE LOGS

BLOCK A   BLOCK B

MAKE 7 COPIES OF THIS TEMPLATE AT 100% TO PAPER PIECE A SMALL QUILT USING YOUR LEFTOVER

SCRAPS FROM BERRY BLUSH. MAKE 6 ROWS OF 6 BLOCKS EACH USING 20 OF BLOCK A AND 16 OF

BLOCK B. REFER TO THE PHOTO AT LEFT TO PLACE THEM FOR THE BARN-RAISING EFFECT.

It is not that artistic power

has left the world,

but that a more rapid life

has developed itself in it,

leaving no time for

deliberate dainty decoration

or labours of love.

— MRS. ORRINSMITH, 1877

SAMPLER

MAJESTIC MOUNTAINS

RATING: *Advanced*

CLASSIC AND CONTEMPORARY BLOCKS: SISTERS CHOICE (OR SNOWFLAKE), WILD GOOSE CHASE,
LOG CABIN, SNOWY SPRUCE, CASCADES CABIN APPLIQUÉ

DESIGNED AND PIECED BY ROXANNE BESMEHN, JEAN MUSICK, NELLIE HARMON OLIVER,
EULA OYALA, JUDY TEAL, VIRGINIA "GINNY" WAGENBLAST, JOANNE WIDME, AND BARBIE WINDSOR.

QUILTED BY LORRIE OBERMEIER OF FOREVER QUILTING, ST. HELENS, OREGON

A challenge for the advanced quilter, this wonderful sampler is a melding of something
old and something new. The old blocks include Wild Goose Chase, Log Cabin, and
Sisters Choice, also known as Snowflake. The quilters gained permission to include a
contemporary block design, Snowy Spruce, from the folks at Electric Quilt. And appliqué
artist Nellie Harmon Oliver designed the centerpiece landscape that anchors the entire
design. It's based on a cabin scene from Oregon's Cascade Mountains. That little nine-
patch quilt on the line is a freeform piece, too—an adorable addition to a stunning quilt.

Finished block size: Varies-see below
Finished quilt size: 100" x 102"

Fabric Requirements

White	1 yard
Light Blue	1¼ yard
Light Green	⅓ yard
Med. Green	1 yard
Light Purple	⅓ yard
Med. Light Purple	½ yard
Med. Purple	½ yard
Med. Dark Purple	½ yard
Dark Purple	¼ yard
Light Gold	¼ yard
Med. Gold	¼ yard
Med. Dark Gold	¼ yard
Dark Gold	¼ yard
Dark Green	Scraps

Red	Scraps
Brown	Scraps
White	Scraps
Purple	Scraps
Blue	19 yards No. 7081-2 - Style 3416 Luminaries (10 yards backing; 8 yards background, sashing, and borders; 1 yard at 2³/₄" strip [bias] binding)

To keep the project manageable, we'll cut, sew, and assemble this big quilt in three separate pieces: SECTIONS A, B, and C, beginning with the upper third of the quilt top, the Snowflakes section.

SECTION A

SISTERS CHOICE (SNOWFLAKES)

DIAGRAM A

Cutting Directions (Based on a 42" wide fabric)

1. From background fabric, cut (4) strips 1¹/₂" x 42", then sub-cut into 88 squares measuring 1¹/₂" x 1¹/₂". Set aside as "X" squares.

2. From background fabric, cut (2) strips 1⁷/₈" x 42", then sub-cut into 44 squares measuring 1⁷/₈" x 1⁷/₈". Set aside as "Y" squares.

3. From the white fabric, cut (4) strips 1¹/₂" x 42", then sub-cut into 99 squares measuring 1¹/₂" x 1¹/₂". Set aside with "X" squares.

4. From white fabric, cut (2) strips 1⁷/₈" x 42", then sub-cut into 44 squares measuring 1⁷/₈" x 1⁷/₈". Set aside with "Y" squares.

Sewing Directions

1. Take fabric for the Y squares and assemble, placing background fabric face-to-face with white fabric. Draw a diagonal line across the square and sew a seam ¹/₄" away from each side of the line. Cut on the line. Press toward the dark and trim off the "ears." Each set of squares will yield (2) half-square triangles. Repeat, making 88 half-square triangles. Chain-piecing will speed your progress.

2. Assemble with solid-color or white squares following Diagram A to make a single block. Make 11 blocks measuring 5¹/₂" x 5¹/₂", unfinished.

Section A Background Fabric Cutting Instructions

1. Cut (2) 2¹/₄" x 5¹/₂" strips for sides
2. Cut (11) 9" x 5¹/₂" blocks to join Snowflake blocks
3. Cut (2) 2¹/₂" x 76¹/₂" strips for top and bottom

Assembling Section A

Join the Snowflakes blocks with background fabric to create Section A as shown in Diagram B. Set aside.

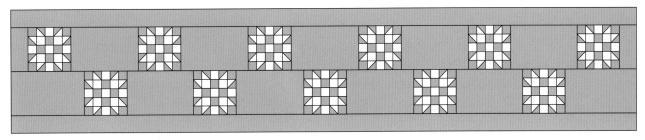

DIAGRAM B

SECTION B

The next section is made up of the following blocks: Snowy Spruce, Flying Geese, and the Cascades Cabin Appliqué. Next we'll work on these, along with cutting the background pieces necessary for Section B.

SNOWY SPRUCE
Cutting and Sewing Directions

Gather a pile of scraps from the background fabric, white, dark green, and brown. Copy the template on pages 68–69 at 300% to use for paper piecing 8 blocks that will measure $6\frac{1}{2}$" x $6\frac{1}{2}$", unfinished.

1. This block is assembled in four units. Use Brown for the tree trunk in Step 1 of Unit A. Use Dark Green fabric scraps for Steps 4, 5, and 8 in Unit A. Use White for Step 10. For all other steps, use the background fabric.

2. In Unit B, use Dark Green for Step 2, and White for Step 3, with background fabric for Steps 1 and 4.

3. In Units D and C, Step 2 White, Step 3 is Dark Green, and the background fabric is used in Steps 1 and 4.

4. Join the four strips to create the single block.

SNOWY SPRUCE TEMPLATE

Make 8 photocopies at 100% to paper piece.

Unit: D

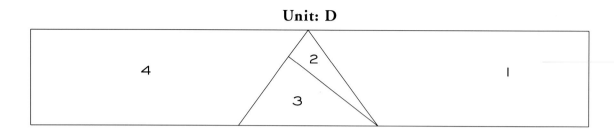

Unit: B

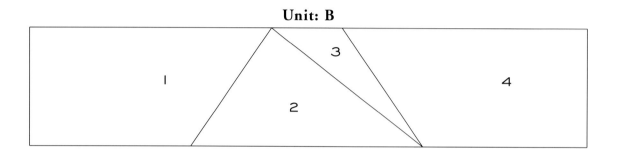

Unit: C

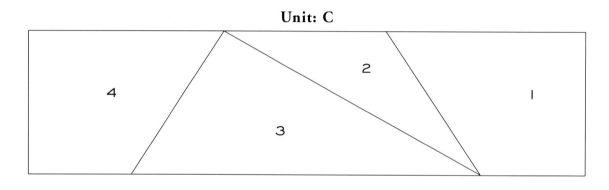

Unit: A

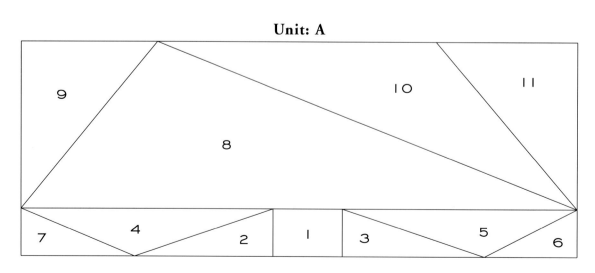

FLYING GEESE

Each Goose measures 6½" x 3½" unfinished. A finished strip of five geese is 6" x 15".

Cutting Directions

Each set makes 4 Flying Geese. Cut 1 set in each of the five lavender/purple fabrics, light to dark. You will make a total of 20 Flying Geese.

1.

For each set:
Sky (background fabric):   Cut (4) 3⅞" x 3⅞" squares
Geese (five shades, light to dark): Cut (1) 7¼" x 7¼" square

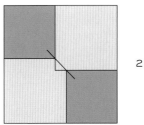

2&3

Sewing Directions *(see Diagram C)*

1. Draw a diagonal line on the wrong side of the four smaller squares. Mark a ¼" stitching line on either side of the diagonal line on both squares. (You will have three lines.)

2. Lay the larger square on the table with the right side up. Place two small squares with the right side down on the large square in opposite corners.

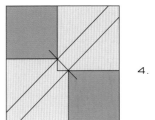

4.

3. Use scissors to clip across the points of the squares where they overlap. This is very important.

4. Sew on the sewing lines you drew in Step 1.

5. Cut this apart diagonally between the sewing lines. This will give you 2 pieces.

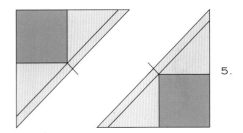

5.

6. Press the seams on both of the above pieces.

7. Add the remaining two small squares to the corner opposite of the triangular pieces on both of the pieces from Step 6.

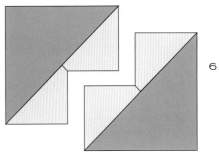

6.

8. Stitch on the lines marked in Step 1. Cut apart on the first diagonal line you drew in Step 1 in this square. Complete this step on both pieces you had in Step 7.

9. Press seams.

10. Repeat through five steps to create 20 Flying Geese.

11. Join your Flying Geese into 4 strips of 5 geese each, moving from light to dark on each strip.

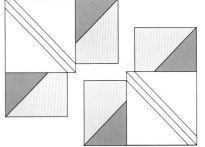

7&8

DIAGRAM C

Copy each page at 300% and join the copies at the broken lines for tracing the design.

CASCADES CABIN APPLIQUÉ

Cutting directions

Cut (1) each of the following shapes:

Light Blue	23" x 24" rectangle	Appliqué background
Light Green	10" x 34" rectangle	Foreground
Dark Green	6" x 21" rectangle	Hills
Gold	4" x 18" rectangle	Cabin
Med. Light Purple	6" x 16" rectangle	Hills
Dark Purple	9" x 9" square	Hills
White	9" x 17" rectangle	Mountains
Blue	8" x 19" rectangle	River

Cut scraps of:

Red	Barn
Dark Gold	Cabin, Clothesline poles, Sawhorse
Med. Gold	Path
Dark & Med. Greens	Trees
Brown	Bear
White with gray	Clouds, Shadows on mountains
Light Purple	Hill
Medium Purple	Hill
Purple	Small quilt
White	Small quilt

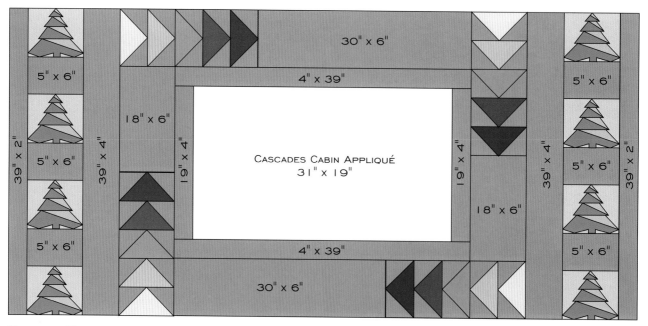

DIAGRAM D

Appliqué Instructions

You can use your favorite appliqué method, such as ironing freezer paper to the back of your fabric, marking directly on the fabric, using a product such as Steam-A-Seam (remembering to reverse the pattern), or choosing machine appliqué (no seam allowance is necessary).

Here's the method that designer Nellie Harmon Oliver used for our sampler quilt:

1. Photocopy the appliqué template on pages 68–69 at 300%, then trace the drawing onto freezer paper.

2. Number the pieces in the order to be sewn, beginning with the background pieces, middle ground, then foreground. Cut out individual pieces.

3. Press on the *right* side of the fabric, and cut around the pieces, allowing a $1/8$" to $1/4$" seam allowance.

4. Needle-turn pieces to background fabric.

5. Save the mini quilt for last. Make the tiniest nine-patch that your fingers and eyes will allow and use a piece of scrap for backing. Place right sides together and stitch around the block leaving space open for turning. Turn and hand stitch it closed.

6. Embroider a clothesline between the poles.

7. Appliqué the tiny quilt to the clothesline. Embroider clothespins.

When finished, trim center appliqué to $19\,1/2$" x $31\,1/2$".

Section B Background Fabric Cutting Instructions

(2) strips $4\,1/2$" x $19\,1/2$"	sides of center appliqué
(2) strips $4\,1/2$" x $39\,1/2$"	top and bottom of center appliqué
(2) strips $6\,1/2$" x $18\,1/2$"	between flying geese on sides
(2) strips $6\,1/2$" x $30\,1/2$"	between flying geese, top and bottom
(2) strips $4\,1/2$" x $39\,1/2$"	inside trees
(6) rectangles $5\,1/2$" x $6\,1/2$"	between trees
(2) strips $2\,1/2$" x $39\,1/2$"	outside trees

Assembling Section B

Join the various blocks and background pieces as shown in Diagram D. Set aside.

SECTION C

LOG CABIN BLOCK

Unfinished measurement: 10 1/2" x 10 1/2"
Make 7 blocks

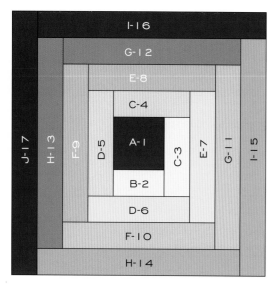

DIAGRAM E

Cutting Directions

Strip width 1 1/2"

Strip length:
A – Cut (7) 2 1/2" x 2 1/2" dark (center square)
B – Cut (7) 1 1/2" x 2 1/2" light
C – Cut (7) 1 1/2" x 3 1/2" dark; (7) 1 1/2" x 3 1/2" light
D – Cut (7) 1 1/2" x 4 1/2" dark; (7) 1 1/2" x 4 1/2" light
E – Cut (7) 1 1/2" x 5 1/2" dark; (7) 1 1/2" x 5 1/2" light
F – Cut (7) 1 1/2" x 6 1/2" dark; (7) 1 1/2" x 6 1/2" light
G – Cut (7) 1 1/2" x 7 1/2" dark; (7) 1 1/2" x 7 1/2" light
H – Cut (7) 1 1/2" x 8 1/2" dark; (7) 1 1/2" x 8 1/2" light
I – Cut (7) 1 1/2" x 9 1/2" dark; (7) 1 1/2" x 9 1/2" light
J – Cut (7) 1 1/2" x 10 1/2" dark

Assemble in order as shown in Diagram E.

Section C Background Fabric Cutting Instructions

(11) 2 1/4" x 10 1/2" rectangles for use in Steps 1, 2, 5, 6, 7, 10, 11, 12, 16, 17, 18

(1) 2 1/4" x 14 1/2" rectangle for use in Step 3

(2) 2 1/4" x 25 1/2" rectangles for use in Steps 8 and 19

(2) 2 1/4" x 37 1/2" rectangles for use in Steps 14 and 21

(1) 11" x 11" square, then sub-cut once diagonally for setting triangles in Steps 24 and 25

(3) 13" x 13" squares, then sub-cut once diagonally for setting triangles in Steps 4, 9, 13, 15, 20 (*You will have one extra*)

(1) 19" x 19" square, then sub-cut once diagonally for setting triangles in Steps 22 and 23

(*Trim triangles to fit after sewing together*)

(2) 4" x 27 1/2" rectangles for left and right borders, Steps 27 and 28

(2) 2 1/2" x 76 1/2" rectangles for top and bottom borders, Steps 29 and 30

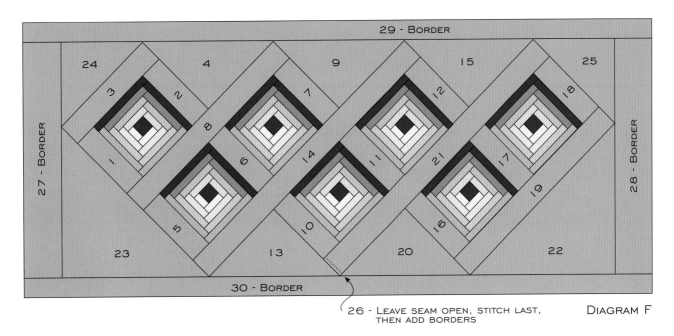

26 - LEAVE SEAM OPEN, STITCH LAST,
THEN ADD BORDERS

DIAGRAM F

Assembling Section C

Join the seven unfinished log cabin blocks to the background fabric, following the assembly steps shown in Diagram F exactly.

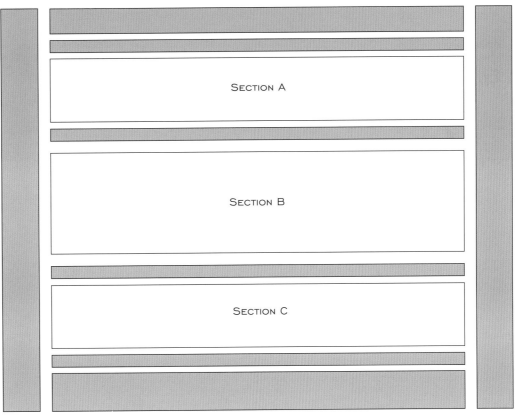

SECTION A

SECTION B

SECTION C

DIAGRAM G

Top Assembly

Finish the top by joining Sections A, B, and C as shown in Diagram G. Layer, quilt as desired, and bind.

Thus is a Needle prov'd an Instrument

Of profit, pleasure, and of ornament.

Which Mighty Queenes have grac'd in hand to take,

And high-borne Ladies such esteeme did make,

That as their Daughters Daughters up did grow,

The Needles Art, they to their children show.

— JOHN TAYLOR [1580-1653]
"THE PRAISE OF THE NEEDLE"

FINISHING TOUCHES

Embroidery

A Crazy Quilt is a perfect place to display your expertise for embroidery stitches. If you're lacking experience or stuck in a rut of Daisy Chains and French Knots, check out a how-to book and expand your stitching repertoire. Jazz up your appliqué work on any quilt with special embellishments.

Choosing the Right Batting

Batting comes in pre-cut sizes for crib, twin, full, queen, or king sizes. Or you can buy it off the roll. It's available in low-, medium-, or high-loft—the higher the loft, the fluffier the areas between quilted lines. That may be great for a baby quilt, but you probably don't want that look on every quilt, so choose accordingly. Also, if you're planning to hand quilt, you'll want batting that doesn't fight your needle. Low loft works best for hand-quilters. Batting can be purchased in polyester only; in a polyester and cotton combination; or in 100% cotton.

Have you pre-washed the fabric? Then you're probably safe with polyester or the combined poly-cotton batting. If your cotton quilt top hasn't been washed, choose 100% cotton batting. When it's washed, the two layers should shrink similarly. But a bad combination could land you with a top that shrinks and batting that doesn't, creating a sea of puckers.

Assembling the Layers

Lap Quilting and Home Machine Quilting. Lucky people have a work surface—at least a dining room table—large enough to lay out a quilt at hip level. Others find themselves crabbing around on the floor, complaining about their knees and backs! Either way works, but using the table is better for smoothing out wrinkles and taping down the backing so everything stays put.

The first step is to lay out the backing, good side down. The backing should extend 4"–6" beyond the raw edge of the quilt top. Smooth out any wrinkles and pay attention to the location of any seams. Ensure that they remain parallel to the edge when the layers are secured. Next lay out the batting, which should also extend 4"–6" beyond the raw edge of the quilt. Finally comes the quilt top. Again, smooth out any wrinkles.

Use your favorite method to secure the three-layer "sandwich." If you are a fan of adhesive sprays, you will spray the individual layers as you lay them out. Hand-quilters often run long basting stitches through the layers, starting with a big X from corner to corner. Next, baste every 5" or so. When the quilt is in the hoop, you'll be glad for the extra effort. Some hand-quilters and most home machine-quilters prefer quilting pins, affixing them every 4"–6" all over the quilt top. And then there are the basting guns that shoot a plastic tie through the layers, a little like the plastic ties on price tags at the department store. These must be clipped out later.

Frame Quilting. Most frames can feed the layers of backing, batting, and quilt top to a central work area for hand quilting. The trick is to make sure each layer is good and square when it is fed onto its own rod.

Long-Arm-Machine Quilting. If your quilt is headed to a professional long-arm-machine quilter, no further assembly is required. You'll simply bring your backing and quilt top to the shop. Usually you can purchase your batting there, but bring your own if you like. You will choose thread color and quilting design with the help of these creative professionals. Don't feel like you have to have all of the answers. They can advise you. It will come back to you with raw edges, ready for you to trim the extra backing and batting, then bind.

Quilting

Hand Quilting. This ageless craft allows quilters to linger with their creations and become even more familiar with every seam. Sure it takes longer, but the companionship of friends, a fresh cup of coffee, and quilt in your lap or on the frame is unbeatable. In addition, there's the joy of magnifying the beauty of your quilt top with your own hand-work. Check out the many books available on hand-quilting patterns and the varied selection of templates and transfer methods. Ask about the best batting for hand quilting.

Machine Quilting. Take a class or apprentice yourself to an experienced home machine-quilter, and discover the pleasures of completing your quilt on your own. The advantages are many: You decide what pattern to use and where. There's no waiting. You can work at your own pace. And your creative mark is visible, not only on the piecework, but also on the quilting. Go beyond stippling and try some new methods.

Long-Arm Quilting. Long-arm-machine quilting is ideal for the person who's in love with designing quilt tops. As soon as one top is done, you're ready to cast your creative eye on the next one. Let somebody else do the quilting! While these small businesses are cropping up everywhere, it seems there are never enough. You'll likely need a reservation for having your quilt professionally finished. Check your local listings for long-arm quilters, and ask around among guild members or quilt shops for recommendations. They can vary widely in expertise and pricing.

Hanging Sleeves

With a sleeve, the weight of a displayed quilt is distributed more evenly across a hanging rod; other methods may place stress on certain points and could cause the quilt to become misshapen. If you want a sleeve, it's best to decide before you bind, but obviously you can always add one later.

Use a coordinating fabric (or contrasting, just for fun), and cut a strip that's 6" wide and 1" wider than the hanging side of your quilt. Fold in the edges on the short sides of the strip and machine stitch a narrow "hem" (about ½" or less). Then fold in half lengthwise, right sides out, place the unfinished edges along the raw edge of the quilt, and machine stitch about ¼" in from the edge. Later, this will be covered with the binding. Finish by hand-stitching the folded edge to the backing. The hanging slat or rod should slip into the sleeve, not behind it.

Binding

Your top has been layered and quilted. Now it's time to trim off the extra backing and batting and prepare for binding. It's not necessary to cut it off exactly at the edge of the quilt top. More importantly, make sure you leave enough of the fluffy stuff to fill out the binding material completely.

I've found that a bias tape maker is a handy tool, but many of my fellow quilters prefer this method for a more durable finished edge: Join pieces to create a 2¼"-wide strip that's as long as the combined lengths of each side of the quilt, plus an extra 3"–4" for good measure. Simply fold the binding in half, good side out, and machine sew the two raw edges to the front of the quilt with a ¼" seam allowance. The seam should be about 1" from the edge. Miter the corners. Now pull the binding flap around to the back and hand stitch it into place, covering the sewing line that you just made.

Labels

Too often quilters are so happy to be finished with their newest quilt that they feign exhaustion—too tired to make a label. Time goes by, you forget the details, and soon you have another anonymous quilt floating around. Take the extra minutes to make a label, even if it's a piece of muslin marked with a fabric pen.

Your label can be as simple or elaborate as you like. Include the date, your name, the name of the person who it's for and/or the quilt's name, city and state, plus any other sweet messages you may want to include.

If you're computer savvy, buy a program to design it on screen and print it out on a specialty fabric sheet with a peel-off back. Artsy types can press a piece of freezer paper to the back of your label fabric to secure it, and use fabric pens to draw, write, embellish in any way. Peel off the paper and stitch into place. How about using an extra block for your label? Embroider the words by hand, by machine, or write with a fabric pen. Have fun with it.

Your Quilt Journal

Take photos of your work while it's in progress and again when it's finished (with you in the picture, too!). You'll cherish these images as the years go by, and more importantly, those who acquire your quilts in the future will know more about the quilt's history. Shop for a photo album with sleeves to hold your photos and fabric scraps. Make sure there's plenty of room to write notes near the photos.

SCRAPBOOK

ABOUT THE QUILTERS

The Columbia River Piecemakers Quilt Guild is an association of forty to fifty quilters who live in Columbia County, Oregon, north of Portland. The group meets monthly to celebrate a love of quilting, learn more about their craft, and encourage each other along the way. They view quilting not only as a personal expression of art, but also as a way to bring comfort to the sick, lonely, or distressed. The guild regularly donates quilts or quilt raffle earnings to women's shelters, senior centers, and needy people in their communities. The Piecemakers plan to auction or donate the quilts in *Fresh Air in the Attic* to benefit select charities throughout the county. Watch for auction information in 2004 at www.classiccottons.com.

▲ KATIE GARMAN CLEVERLY USED FRESH COLOR CHOICES AND KITTY APPLIQUÉS (IN VARIOUS STAGES OF NAUGHTINESS) TO ENHANCE THE OLD SNOWBALL-AND-NINE-PATCH STANDARD.

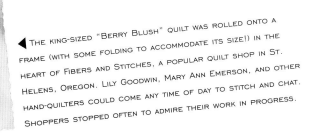

▲ EDNA MORSE IS A CONSISTENT BLUE-RIBBON WINNER AT THE COLUMBIA COUNTY FAIR WITH HER BEAUTIFULLY STITCHED MINIATURE QUILTS. AFTER SEEING THE FINISHED KING-SIZED LOG CABIN QUILT, SHE ASKED, "DO YOU HAVE ANY SCRAPS LEFT OVER?" AND VOILA! EDNA DELIVERED A PICTURE-PERFECT, DOLL-SIZED LOG CABIN QUILT.

▲ AMANDA MCFERON'S SKILLFUL USE OF COLOR IN AN ON-POINT DESIGN CREATED A PICTURE OF MOTION IN "FEATHERED FRENZY." ONE YEAR AFTER LEARNING TO QUILT, AMANDA ENTERED ANOTHER QUILT IN THE COUNTY FAIR'S QUILTING COMPETITION AND WALKED AWAY WITH BEST IN SHOW.

▲ CHRIS STANSBURY AND CATHY LUNDBERG PUT THEIR EMBROIDERY SKILLS TO WORK AFTER PIECING "GONE CRAZY." THE FINISHED QUILT IS A FEAST FOR THE EYES WITH TINY DETAILS RUNNING THROUGH EVERY BLOCK.

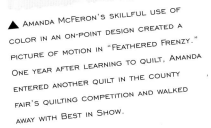

◀ THE KING-SIZED "BERRY BLUSH" QUILT WAS ROLLED ONTO A FRAME (WITH SOME FOLDING TO ACCOMMODATE ITS SIZE!) IN THE HEART OF FIBERS AND STITCHES, A POPULAR QUILT SHOP IN ST. HELENS, OREGON. LILY GOODWIN, MARY ANN EMERSON, AND OTHER HAND-QUILTERS COULD COME ANY TIME OF DAY TO STITCH AND CHAT. SHOPPERS STOPPED OFTEN TO ADMIRE THEIR WORK IN PROGRESS.

The "Snowy Spruce" block on page 66 is from Sew Precise 1 & 2 by the Electric Quilt Company, published with permission. The "Sisters Choice" block first appeared in *The Romance of the Patchwork Quilt in America*, by Carrie A. Hall and Rose G. Kretsinger (Caldwell, Idaho: Caxton Printers, 1935). Reprinted by Dover Publications in March 1989. Both editions are out of print. The quotation on page 32 is from *Aunt Jane of Kentucky*, by Eliza Calvert Hall, © 1907, reissued by the University Press of Kentucky in 1995.

LIBRARY OF CONGRESS CATALOGING-IN-PUBLICATION DATA
Fresh air in the attic : welcome makeovers for 7 classic quilts / Edited
by Tricia Brown.
    p. cm.
 ISBN 1-55868-798-X (softbound : alk. paper)
 1. Patchwork—Patterns. 2. Quilting. 3. Patchwork quilts. I. Brown, Tricia.
 TT835.F747 2004
 746.46—dc22
              2003026334

WestWinds Press®
An imprint of Graphic Arts Center Publishing Company
P.O. Box 10306, Portland, Oregon 97296-0306
502-226-2402; www.gacpc.com

President: Charles M Hopkins
Associate Publisher: Douglas A. Pfeiffer
Editorial Staff: Timothy W. Frew, Kathy Howard, Jean Andrews, Jean Bond-Slaughter
Production Staff: Richard L. Owsiany, Susan Dupere
Editor: Tricia Brown
Photographer: Trish Reynolds
Designer: Andrea Boven Nelson, Boven Design Studio, Inc.
Proofreaders: Nancy Gates and Linda Nelson

Printed in China